THE PORTAGE POETRY SERIES

SERIES TITLES

Lake, River, Mountain
Mark B. Hamilton

Talking Diamonds
Linda Nemec Foster

Poetic People Power
Tara Bracco (ed.)

The Green Vault Heist
David Salner

There is a Corner of Someplace Else
Camden Michael Jones

Everything Waits
Jonathan Graham

We Are Reckless
Christy Prahl

Always a Body
Molly Fuller

Bowed As If Laden With Snow
Megan Wildhood

Silent Letter
Gail Hanlon

New Wilderness
Jenifer DeBellis

Fulgurite
Catherine Kyle

The Body Is Burden and Delight
Sharon White

Bone Country
Linda Nemec Foster

Not Just the Fire
R.B. Simon

Monarch
Heather Bourbeau

The Walk to Cefalù
Lynne Viti

The Found Object Imagines a Life: New and Selected Poems
Mary Catherine Harper

EXILE IS HOME

Each of the poems in Elvis Alves's new collection is a crossroads between self and history, love and obligation, faith and grief. Each bears the revelations of an individual both lost and found, at large in the diaspora, in the streets of Brooklyn or on a commuter train, in a coffee shop, a cab, a bridge. The defining notion of "story" is constantly evoked—the human mystery flickers out of the rush of urban and professional life. Alves's language is spare and precise. Not a word is wasted, which means that each word bears the weight both of meaning and of our experience of meaning, which duality is the remit of both poetry and prayer. It is impossible, I think, to read these poems and not be moved by their human freight, the hope, the pain, the faith, the anxiety, and the experience of mystery that drive individual destinies.

—TERENCE CULLETON
author of *A Tree and Gone*

Alves covers a lot of ground in a collection where the sacred and the profane, the downtrodden and the queens, and redemption and spirituality pulse behind the specter sounds of the jazz greats like memory uncovered. A foot planted in two cultures shows us survival and living at its finest. Alves is a memory-maker, a risk-taker and his poems are a guide along the way. *Exile Is Home* is a Brooklyn fever dream with a sturdy heartbeat and an associative memory of belonging.

—MICHELLE REALE
author of *Season of Subtraction*

EXILE IS HOME

poems

Elvis Alves

CORNERSTONE PRESS
UNIVERSITY OF WISCONSIN-STEVENS POINT

Cornerstone Press, Stevens Point, Wisconsin 54481
Copyright © 2025 Elvis Alves
www.uwsp.edu/cornerstone

Printed in the United States of America.

Library of Congress Control Number: 2025940337
ISBN: 978-1-960329-96-7

Cornerstone Press titles are produced in courses and internships offered by the Department of English at the University of Wisconsin–Stevens Point.

DIRECTOR & PUBLISHER
Dr. Ross K. Tangedal

EXECUTIVE EDITORS
Jeff Snowbarger, Freesia McKee

EDITORIAL DIRECTOR
Brett Hill

SENIOR EDITOR
Ellie Atkinson

PRESS STAFF
Paige Biever, Aja Woolley, Alex Diaz, Brianna Loving, Leo Poskoum, Eva Nielsen
Sophie McPherson, Sam Bjork, Madison Schultz, Autumn Vine, Allison Lange

for Maleeha and Malcolm

ALSO BY ELVIS ALVES:

This Is What I Know

Blackfish

Black/White: We Are Not Panic (Pandemic) Free

I Am No Battlefield But A Forest Of Trees Growing

Ota Benga

Bitter Melon

POEMS

Faith Holds Fast to Uncertainties, Without Knowing

(Speaker One) You should tell me what you are thinking?
(Speaker Two) Is that the only way I can be freed?

—Gayl Jones, *Asylum*

Forge Something Into Being

Papa Legba

Walks with a
stick and moves
quick.

Papa Legba...is strong.
Guards the
graveyard and
gates of heaven.

Papa Legba
works hard.

Be careful he
hits you with
his stick.

If this happens,
he will welcome
you in the
afterlife.

Primordial Orbits (Arrival)

for Cheryl Boyce-Taylor

We land on new shores. Night is in our heads.
The call to march will come, but for now
we hear nothing, even though noise surrounds us.

We are swelling with the tide. Sweating a history
that refuses to leave us.

Night and day beg us stay and grow. Become
strong. Forge something into being, a conglomerate
of selves wading through waves.

Birdsong

I was raised in the wilderness that was Brooklyn.
My father befriended the junkies that hung out at the
corner of our block.

They waxed history while pigeons meddled at their
feet, pecking at garbage colored with empty crack
vials.

Sometimes one would swallow a vial. When this happened,
its head would fall to the ground first, with tail
raised as if sending a message to God.

Some birds take flight w/o noise.

Preparing for Mass

She leads us into the church at the heart of the
South Bronx, whose thick doors are unable
to keep cigarette smoke from entering the sanctuary.

The nuns that live in the adjacent convent say at night
they shoo people away from its steps.

In the church, we prepare for the next day's mass.
My colleague explains the Eucharist to the students,
as if they don't know what it is.

"You will eat the actual body of Christ," she says.
I bow my head and pray for an understanding that
surpasses all understanding.

I See w/ Eyes Clear

for Maleeha

The stories I tell you must remain in your
heart and mind. Share them but do so with people you trust.

And even so, don't share the whole thing unless
they betray and give away your secrets. Somethings are

not for sale. Your privacy and dignity are in this category.
I know that you are bold. Courage is on your shoulders.

I see with eyes clear. Never let go of who you are. Stand
strong and carry on.

The Bridge

Rollins practices scales on the Williamsburg Bridge.
His fingers on fire in the cold air.

No one recognizes him, nor his saxophone.
They are oversized by the city even though they
are a duo to contend with.

Rollins likes being unseen. He wants his music
to be more known than him.

Music is his fate. He knows this on the bridge.

Harriet Tubman

You could have freed a thousand more slaves if they knew
they were slaves. I ask my students what freedom means
to them?

One said the ability to roam widely without the
supervision of his parents. Where would he go? Red Lobster.
You have Red Lobster money? yells the smartest student in the class.

There's an eruption of laughter. Then silence. In the silence, I
think of black men in chain gangs on Southern roads, supervised
by white men with guns. This was after slavery.

What is freedom to the unfreed who has never tasted it? I think
of you, Harriet, and your bravery and I remember the laughter
that preceded the silence. How it filled the room like clouds
in the sky. A taste of joy. A sign of freedom.

Dreams

1. are made of silver and gold in the belly of a whale
moving to land full speed ahead of the storm that catches
and devours it.

2. One night a bird flew into my head then fell on the
ground dead but not before screaming *hallelujah*.

3. The old couple lived in the top part of the house until
the visitors came and moved them to the first floor where

they escaped to the street an inch from the shore and
waded in water with cries of freedom.

4. You move on to the next big thing by enjoying
the small in the present.

I Sign My Life Over to You

for Dana

We go to the court building on 161st Street.
Marriage license is in the basement.

We completed half the application online but
wait over an hour to sign a paper that says we intend to
marry.

I see for the first time the hyphenated last name of my
wife-to-be, the ink slowly soaking into paper like
the reality of marriage.

Rastaman Vibration

He walks around the avenue but goes nowhere.
He wears a crown of hair, the length of which
touches the ground. Ganja smoke stays on his
clothes. He has a knife in his pocket to protect
his profit. He is a street pharmacist. Transplant
from the islands. More than fifty years in this
foreign land. He is no fool. It is just that hard
times have found a home in his life. He was on
the road to success until he threw away the comb
and start lick the pipe, his father says. That was
years ago. Both parents dead. His woman and
children left for Texas. He has no friend in this
concrete jungle. He begs for bread and gets by
with sales from the herb. Police put him in jail
many times. But he hugs the corner and prays
for positive vibration to come his way.

Politricks as Usual

He steals truth from the hearts of people who
blindly follow him.

Their lives ruined by the motive of divide and
conquer.

Mobilize the mass by telling them what
they want to hear. The evangelist and
politician know this.

They are cut from the same cloth. A pulpit
is a podium.

A king's crown has blood on it. Never aspire
to this. Instead, move from what you are told.

Exile Is Home

Georgetown, Guyana

The city, named for a British king, is crumbling.
My mother thinks we are being followed by a

woman in the supermarket. She is on the lookout
for robbers. We are tourists in our native land. I

wonder if there is a price on our backs. We escape
to the streets with bags of groceries in hands. I lead

the charge even though I don't know where we are
going. The crowd pushes us forward. A man lies stiff

on the street. Is he dead? I ask the driver. Keep walking,
he says. The smell of sewage is in the air. I make a

promise not to come back again. I know I am lying. I
tell the part about the sewage to a parent at a suburban

football game. His family too escaped Guyana.
There are beautiful countries in the world, why would

I go there? He says to me. He is telling me his
resolution of not returning. My mother and I stay in

Belladrum, the village where she was born, miles from
Georgetown, and where there are more cows on the road

than people at night. The people show up, especially on
Sunday, when they walk to church dressed in colorful clothes

as if on parade. How did we get here? The answer lies in
my father preceding us to New York City, picking up the

habits of smoking and drinking along the way. He tells me that
one day he just quit cold turkey. Threw the cigarette on the floor

and walked away. He stores a cold beer in the fridge for Friday.
Celebration for the end of the work week. A remnant of the time

he downed Old English 40 Oz's while my siblings and I played
at the playground in our Brooklyn neighborhood. He stays in New York

while my mother and I travel. Visit family and hear their stories.
A cousin lives in a house without lights. Her daughter finds a
way to study and pass her exams. We are proud of her. My
mother presses a few dollar notes to her mother's palm

as we leave their home. Another relative's husband is dying
of cancer. We make sure that he visits the doctor at least once

while we are there, knowing that the visit is one too few. I go
to the village where I was born. A young lady tells me that I have

the face of her deceased father. I do not know how to take this,
even though, yes, we are relatives. Another hugs me and invites

me to attend a party for his nuptials. I feel welcome. But not for
long because the leaving must happen. A world away from here

calls me to its shores. My mother and I land in New York City. We
drive to her home in silence, except for the chimes on her cellphone
announcing incoming messages—it was off for the last two weeks.

My journey continues to Pennsylvania where I talk to a parent at a football
game about the smell of sewage in Georgetown. I know there is more to say.

There is the return.

Half Nelson

after Miles Davis

Take five.

He is below
the point of
growth.

Relax, nobody is
making fun of you.

Strong mouth.
Big heart.

These compensate
for height.

Don't go, man.

Why you mad?

Take five.

Let Nelson blow
his steam.

He'll be back
to hit the bass

with all he's got.

Conspiracy

Take this ship and
sail to a land awaiting
your presence before
you were born.

Before the heavens
declared your name
on earth.

Some say never ask
for what you can't
handle.

The ax is sharp enough
to cut the wind.

The moon reads minds—

center of the universe
conspiring to bring you
what is for you.

African Queen

for Aunt Madge and the Britton Sisters

Purple woman.
Royal woman.
Dressed to impress,
express yourself.
The universe looks
at you, and smiles.
Full of yourself.
The moon talks sweet
talk when you pass by.
You are a star.
Shine bright.
Leave and come
again.
Come again to
leave.
You are a queen.
Empress.
African beauty.
Mother to sons
and daughters
of royal blood.

The Universe Is a Multi-verse

Never lose your voice in the writing
because the missing voice is your
voice. It haunts the page, wants to
be heard like a child crying in the
wilderness. And is the answer to
Langston's what happens to a dream
deferred? The universe is a multi-verse.
The planets its chapters. Humans are
sentences used to tell stories.
What do you bring to the table?
What is your story? After all, life
is an investment in self.

More Today Than Yesterday

after Charles Earland

The organ drives this groove.
Wait for the hit and you'll be

on your knees.

Please music, let me live free.
The gods make their home in

the head. Music has the power
to overpower them.

A bombardment of sounds. Taste
it. Be it. Know that life is a gift

you are wrapped in.

Eternal Knowledge

People walk w/o looking at each other.
To look is to acknowledge. I see you as
you see me. But they do not care about this.

The girl with water on skin asks her mother
for ice. The mother tells her to look at the sky.

There are dreams there. People too can fly
with the right mind.

At night, birds see with eyes shut. They listen
to the wind against the windows of their ears,
always ready to take flight when the time is right.

I am calling out to the walkers to pay attention,
not just to where they are going, but who go w/
them and who cannot go.

Revelation is to know that what is known is
always unfolding.

Trees Save Lives

His cries do not wake her from the American Dream. She looks out the window to see him lying and wailing on rocks. She turns from the spectacle to pay attention to her other boyfriend—an American—on the phone. And his promise to fly her to New York City soon. He swallows the rocks. They turn into trees that sprout from his body. Watered by tears, they grow fast with thick leaves that lash against the window. The progression of the spectacle, even though impressive, fails to budge her from the phone and voice on its other end, promising a new home. Birds arrive and build nests on the limbs of the trees, before flying away in time to miss the storm that uproots everything in its path, including the trees. These turn to rafts that ferry people to safety.

Made in DR

Backroom or basement serves as operating room,
the newspaper reports after an accident, explosion.

A classmate drew a Dominican Republic flag in
my yearbook. He also wrote the word platanos with
dark, thick letters above it, in the name of pride.

That was '98. Along the way, I have learned bits
about the country and its people. A student once
said to me that her father told her there's no African
in her blood, even though her skin begs to differ.

Africa, too, is in food, music, and religion. But this
poem is not about that (or, maybe it is).

What is made in the Dominican Republic carries no
labels.

Behind the wall of aesthetics is a face that wants to
welcome the world. Therein lies beauty.

The ass worked on, tucked to comply with desire,
has the potential to implode. After all, what is done
in the dark comes to light.

Speak Life Into What You Want
Out of Life

Love and Such

The road leads to the river, where on summer days
lovers meet late in the evening to remind themselves that time
can go slow if they allow it.

The great moon once had children who grew too big and
disappeared because of this. No one knows where they went
but when a child is born, a moon is born.

I am calling out to the seekers to keep seeking. Say a prayer for
the journey and hold strong to it. You give birth to goals by moving
forward.

Positive Vibration

Speak life into
what you want
out of life.

Carry your dreams
in your spirit. Allow
them to fly.

Pray often. Meditate
on everything. The
mind is a vessel that
travels and reflects.

Stand strong
in the storms of
life. They too
shall pass.

Have fun.
Celebrate life
with every breath.

Saint Coltrane

Lost in the stars, any sound means life.
Humanity pulls, as it grows, from the unknown.
What title you give it wears away into oblivion.

Shine as wisdom's incisive cut—know this above
all else.

Music is a spaceship. It travels beyond the ears,
and into the heart. Into the soul.

Dig there with might. Find what you may, there.
Dance with the rhythm of life.

Out of life's chaos, create rhythm instead of order.
This will help you move along—a path, a journey—

or something of the kind.

Pray to Saint Coltrane on the way. He who knows
joy and pain—they are in his music.

Choice

There is no heart here. If there is one, it beats irregularly.
What wakes to the call of the day meets the same fate as he

who refuses to rouse from sleep, a dream or body holding in
place that whose fate lies somewhere else but draws close with

the passing of time. The heart that beats on its own, or because
it is tugged, lends a paradigm that obstructs the truth
its subject begs to know.

Yes, the heart can be a shallow pond. Or a river or
ocean that knows the depth of love.

The Fire in My Brother

My brother tells me he does not see skin color. That he sees credentials and (work) performance. He says this after I tell him blacks are last to be hired and first to be fired.

My brother runs after the taxicab with a baseball bat in hand. He is on the Westside Hwy, near the Brooklyn Bridge Ext. A white man in the taxicab (moments before) spits in his face. He had cut off the cab. The white man is the passenger. Words are exchanged between him and my brother. Then the spit happens. And my brother running after the cab with the bat. The cab cannot go anywhere because of traffic. My brother catches up with it. And smashes the back window with the bat, where the passenger sits. His spit still on my brother's face. The police show up and arrest my brother. After a night in jail, he is slapped with a court date which he shows up to. The white passenger does not show up to witness against my brother. The judge lets him go because of this—with a fine.

Years later, my brother tells me about credentials and performance. I want him to say *I feel your pain*. I wonder what happened to the fire that was in him the night he ran after the taxicab with a baseball bat in hand.

Imhotep

I can teach everything
because everything is
teachable. A subject is
a subject. That is what
it is and nothing else.
Read the lines of my
palms. They run to
the beginning of time
and back. Ask the
original people whose
bones they collect
and learn to walk into
the unknown that
became them. There
is a world that science
cannot claim. Nor religion,
or anything else. It
is on my tongue, a
village that remembers
its origins.

I Miss

The smell of sea on skin.
The kiss of a rising sun.
Birds that serenade with songs.
People who carry the earth's energy,
and moons in their eyes.
Trees that give life, heavy with
fruits that fall from the sky
like stars. All that is green and
nothing in-between. Life removed
from the city.

A Bird in Hand Is Better Than Two in Bushes

The bird that flies from the stronghold leaves a trail
of feathers. Its wings dash through the sky
like lightning, warning and reminding that nature is a
force not to be reckoned with.

A beached whale brings news from its home: you are
destroying me. If I could, I would fly into the bushes
out of your hand.

Not everyone survives what holds them to place.
In the night the breeze sings of freedom that calls
forth the day.

Below the turbulence is peace, unswayed by life's
wont to capture and slay what is in sight. We must remember
this, and not turn from it, because it is all that we have.

Quiet Storm

I wake to
>music on the streets. Car horns
>blasting noise beyond a level I am
>comfortable with.

Many moons from now,
>I will stand in your heart and learn
>to swim to safety. Or another shore
>where people recognize me as
>their own and I feel at home.

I sit in a state of
>bewilderment with all that bewilders me.
>I am calm in the midst of the storm.
>I am a quiet storm.

For Victims of Natural Catastrophes

We cross the river to the other side where a mother
and child wait for the sun before going forward.

The new day a promise fulfilled to them. And us. So we
celebrate life every day because a catastrophe can

happen without a moment's notice. Uprooting.
To transport the will where it does not want to go.

A stubbornness unfamiliar only in its familiarity,
like a counterpart that is part of the whole.

Life happens with intrusions. It is true that every-
thing breaks and needs fixing. An answer that precedes

the question that births it. There is a fate
that becomes you and that you need to make

a home of, with walls of hope that let love in.

The Night James Brown Saved Boston

I forgot my black card that night. Left it in Augusta, Georgia.
That's what happens when you're young and got money on
your mind. But not all white folks are evil. And Boston is a
beautiful city. Why riot? Dr. King was a good man. They
shouldn't have killed him. That was '68. I understood the people's
anger. But I had a show to do. I walked on stage and told the
people to save Boston. I pleaded with my songs. Performed my ass
off. At the end of the night, everyone was too tired from dancing to
riot. Music saved the day. The night. But I was wrong. I should have
let them burn that shit down and start from scratch. If you want me to
explain why, you don't know the pain of the black man.

King of Pop

for Michael Jackson

He moonwalks into our hearts on a box that sits
staring at us as we stare at it, dumbfounded. This
word does not mean that we are dumb. It means
that we are able to feel with our entire body. That
we swallow the stars with the rest of the universe
and dream of the impossible becoming possible
simply by being us.

His feet are golden. Ancient as the pyramids,
they hide secrets like light in crevices on our
skin—a dark that unfolds with mysteries,
things unknown only in their knowing.

There is more to the King of Pop. A title
that bleeds truth, a phrase that spells words
begging to be reached by sound of feet sliding,
moving across floors and audiences captivated
by the moves, down to the bones in the toes—
accustomed to nothing holding them back.

A pop only a king can make, and that draws
us back to reality, that we are sitting in the
room with a television broadcasting something
beyond our control.

Believer

I am no longer the self searching for meaning
because I am the meaning searched for.

I want to bring to form all that calls my name
to its breasts.

A longing to sleep with peace and yet live to know
what comes next in all flavors and levels of
understanding.

I carry a dream with me around my head and
in my heart. It betrays the need to live more
lives than is human, to go beyond

the possible and acquaint self with the
impossible.

I am a believer. A lover of self and all else.

Unfinished Woman

after artwork by Jacqueline Bishop

I

We meet for coffee at a midtown café.
She tells me he hits her. I call him bastard
and plead that she gets a divorce,
call the cops, or kill him. She says it is in
the works. The works? A divorce, she says.
I hold and rub her hands. I feel the earth's
crust breaking beneath them. She carries
a load no one wishes for. She ends the date
by saying that she loves him and that he
understands her. I shake my head in disgust.
She cries. Gets up and walks to the subway.
I do not chase after her this time. I sit. Drink
my coffee. And wonder when I will see her
again.

II

I see them at the café, not far from the seat where
I sit pretending to read a book. She cries. Gets
up. And walks to the A train. I follow her uptown.
She gets off in Harlem. Buys flowers at the flower
shop. She turns around and catches me staring at
her. We hold hands and walk home.
We make love into the afternoon.

III

You might say that I am a villain, but I am a
lady and not all ladies are villains. The guys
I see want to see me. I make up stories that
I tell them. This is what you get from a
struggling actor in a city of struggling actors.
And high rent. The guy I met up with earlier

is a friend. His name is John.
A common name among common
names. He comes from money.
The other guy is a detective. He likes to follow
me around. See if I am telling the truth
about the dates that I go on (I never do).
It is a crazy world and I am in the middle of it.
Here I am, baby, take me as I am.

In Contempt of Fate

Who blaze the path for me as I search for God?
I have come this far by faith. *Only?* What other
ingredients add to my will, allow my eyes to
stay on the prize:

> Of survival,
> climbing the ladder of knowledge
> to build a secure nest. No longer a
> self in a world of selves. Tied with the knot

of marriage and child, I am guilty of wishing to float
with the days as in years past. But I must not stop here.

It is not possible to hold fate in contempt or a chokehold
that squeezes life out of it.

I rest, swing with the mind from this to that, and make of
these days what may.

Cycle

He peddles the way old men peddle, back bent in that
knowing way that nothing can topple what was born

to survive. His thoughts are filled with the next move. How
to gather all that he knows into commerce.

After all, life in the city is not fun without money. He tells himself
this while thinking about where he is going.

He gets there. Dismounts. Gives his love a hug. She is with child.
They eat their fill like people do when hungry.

He offers to pay. She refuses. He pays. He hops on the bike and
leaves her with movements inside of her.

Redemption

Waves are in my head.
I watch the ocean at night.
A turbulent life is not begged
for but is given by the hand
of fate. Redemption stays far,
afraid to come close. In this
bed of blues, flowers will one
day bloom. This is the hope
that I carry, that carries me.

Meet Me in the City

after Junior Kimbrough

Nobody wants to leave home unless home is
where the blues stay.

My bed is empty where you used to sleep.

There is a hole in my pocket. My money seems to
have run off with you.

I hear there's work at the factory in the city, but
I am too old to be standing
                    all day long,
                    all night long.

Plus, the war left a bullet in my back.

Why you leave me, girl?
Please tell me why. Why you up and
leave me, girl?

Meet me in the city. Me and my guitar.
I'll sing you the blues.

Detroit

Life has to be better than waking up early to catch
the bus and stand in a cold building assembling parts
of a car I can't afford to drive.

But mouths need feeding and I have a couple at home.
My daddy did the same—walked through rain and snow
to feed us. He had no rest. Doctors pumped his chest until

he took his last breath. I picked up his habit; smoke cigarette
to kill stress. But stress is something that lives with me. A
byproduct of human activities. Perhaps manufactured by
accident. In any case, it is here. I am trying to deal with it.

Control it to the best of my ability. It is killing me, along
with the cigarettes. Why can't I quit? Who dealt me this hand
and what am I to do with it?

Sometimes these questions have no answer. I search for God
knows what. A piece of land. Shelter. Food on the table. Without
breaking my back. Without passing through the days and not enjoying
life.

Revelation: On the way to work

He waits for the train to arrive after one departs.
He is running late to work. The boss has it out
for him.

He sees a homeless man and thinks that he can
be him. He is one paycheck away from being on
the streets.

He sits. A woman joins him. Time passes. The train
comes. Empty. He continues to sit. The woman
nudges him. "No. I am not getting on."

He walks out of the train station as the train pushes
forward. He walks along the avenue. The wind is
on his back. People pass him. He walks. This time
briskly.

He catches up to others. He does not know where to go.
All he knows is that he has to keep moving. This is what
he tells himself. Just then a man taps him on the shoulders.

"Are you okay, buddy? You look out of it." He does not
answer but smiles.

The sun is shining. The wind blows. This is the Windy
City, he says to himself and ponders how it is
to be on the train on the way to work.

Again, I Bend with the Wind

The insanity of it all grates my mind.
I see the sky with eyes of an eagle.

Something calls my name in the dark.
The light of it—everything has light—is
beyond comprehension.

In the climb, we sacrifice the self, I tell
myself. There is nothing as progress. Life
simply happens, simply at times.

I cool my wits. My mouth spits words that
beg for a home on a page. Everything collapses.

I float with the day, call out for more than
what I already bare.

In time, my progeny will write their names on
slates, evidence that I am still here though gone.

Faith Holds Fast to Uncertainties,
Without Knowing

The Search for Home

We escape to find space to
settle the mind. Where is
home away from home?
There, relief abounds and
sleep is not a stranger. In
this land, birds sing sweet
songs. The seasons are
long and mellow. Mother
nature, too, can learn to
behave—somewhere far
from here.

The Long History of Genocide

Touching land with toes is like
returning to a home you never left.

It is like returning to a home you never
left because the leave taking was one of

necessity. You were priced out of your
neighborhood. The newcomers feel that

it belongs to them. That it was always
theirs for the taking, was just waiting

for their arrival. Columbus and
his crew took land from the natives as if

it was always theirs for the taking, was just
waiting for their arrival. They plant flags,

cast spells with a new language, and decimate
with diseases. The land was always theirs for

the taking, they believed. And they did take.
Gold to Europe. Tobacco. Cotton. Sugar. Bodies.

The land has a way of remembering. Humans easily
forget. They call Columbus a hero, build statues

of him, when in reality he was taken back to
Spain after his third voyage bound in chains—

appropriate uniform for a criminal. Murderer.
But who is listening? Who is reading history?

What Is the Sun Made of?

Everything that floats in its face.
Black skin that reflects its rays. Home.
Native land. A dream fulfilled, at last.
Whatever it needs to feed on, grow
with. Hotness. Not just any hotness.
A will of its own. Never sweetness.
Everything that floats in the face
before dying, before coming alive.
Recyclables. Dust. Heavenly things.
Totally self-made. Everything that
calls it home. My native land. The
land where I was born but did not
grow up in. Distant countries.
Regions waiting to be reached,
like my native land.

Darwin's Nightmare

The students understand Trickle-down economics.
What poses the most challenge is the actual living
out of ideas of fairness, justice, the sharing of power,
or doing something with the affect of love. They
do not know how to take themselves out of the picture
and see from the perspective of the other, especially
when it is different.

We quarrel about what is right. How it differs from the
wrong. They hardly ask for explanation. They want to
make a point and have others follow it. Have me follow
it. I remind them that I am the teacher. That they need
to respect me as I respect them. That I care for them.
I see the good in them. I say these things and think
why can't they see these things in me?

On the ride home, I think of the oppressed making
excuses for the oppressors. *Nobody in the world,*
nobody in history, has ever gotten their freedom
by appealing to the moral sense of the people
who are oppressing them, says Assata Shakur.
I snap out of it. Focus on the road. I leave school
behind when I enter the door and see my daughter's
eyes. Her smile. She sees me.

In the morning, on my drive to work, I pray for
strength to survive another day.

We Black

The sun courses through our skin.
We are builders of creation.
The original people, blueprint for
the rest of humanity. We black and
that is a fact. To create is our destiny.
We black like magic or tar that covers
everything. We are black power. Believe
that.

The Killer Rides Again

for Jacob Miller

Is it not so that life goes?
The killer rides again on rhythm
and beats—a free man is not an easy
feat.

He rides into the horizon.
He rides with a heavy load.

The tenement yard is too hard
a life for him, even a dog cannot
survive there.

Everything Was Imagined Before Existence

The mind has gone missing, again. They are
searching for it. I am along for the ride
but do not know where I am going. We are going.

Brooklyn streets have my name. They keep calling
me to them, just when I want to pull away. This is
what is meant by a force field. An addiction or something
worth escaping.

I leave and chase dreams as they chase me. I am disappearing
into oblivion with time, in time.

No man is an island unless he sees himself as one or begets
one of himself.

Hurry, come rescue me. Find me in the crevices of a world
built by imagination.

Ras Socrates

He begs for nothing. Teaches everything, including
Astrology and Geology, for free. Babylon's soldiers
come around. Call him *dirty* and *insubordinate.*
He curses them in Selassie I's name and licks the pipe to
bless the air, ganja in the brain. They ambush him
at night. Bullets everywhere. He fights and runs away
to fight again.

Where Will You Run?

Worlds crumble and are born with
the space of time expanding like
water in a growing ocean.

Snowflakes beat on windows,
begging to enter warmth.

Chirping birds are absent.
The lesson of their silence long
forgotten.

Some call this the end. Others
see a beginning. Whatever it is,

we cannot turn from but must seek
the knowing.

Bend Down Low, Let Me Tell You What I Know

(She speaks)

I know you. Do you know me?

Many men follow you. Do they know
why?

Dirt sleeps on your sleeves.
Your hair keeps the wind.

Have you eaten?

What exactly is your name?
Who is your master?

Why do they call you rabbi when
you shun the temple?

My questions find a home on your
face. Your mouth's a closed tomb.

You know what is happening here. Where
this is going. I can tell by your eyes. They
say compassion, want me to listen.

But before I do, why are your feet dry?

(She speaks)

Last night, your friend was in my
bed.

He is in the fields, plucking grain
and talking with the Pharisees.
It's the Sabbath.

He sees us and shoots me a glance.
Probably wondering what I am
telling you. If it is about him.

I did not get his name. Am I
the only one with shame?

(He speaks)

I see him watch us talk
at the well.

You are accustomed to the
gaze. I am growing into it.

How do you manage?
How do you keep from
breaking apart under
the looks?

You sense I am different.
Am I?

I will quench your thirst.
Not with water.

You want to know
more than what life offers,

while looking at my feet.

Bomb

I am no lyrical machinery.
I am a bomb exploding beyond
your mental capacity. Fading
into the dark, you cannot hold
me back. I am Noah's Ark lost
in the storm of life but confident
in finding the way to light.

Diabetes

I feel guilty when I give my father food to eat. He is diabetic.
Rice, chicken, wine—everything (it seems) turns into sugar.

His body cannot take it. I am afraid of what diabetes
brings. What it takes. My phobia is that of missing
limbs. I do not know when this began. But I have held it close

for years. A secret. I remember telling a former girlfriend about
the fear when I was in graduate school and a guy with a missing

leg was hired to work alongside me in the mailroom. I did work-
study then. I was fixated by the titanium leg that he, I forgot his

name, wore like a badge, leaving it out to be seen when the weather
was hot and he had on shorts. I got to know the guy. We talked about
everything—politics, religion, cars—except about his leg. I refused.

Did not know how to bring it up. Instead, I made up stories to explain it
away. He stepped on a bomb in Vietnam. But he was too young to have foug

in the Vietnam War. Another story was that he was a truck driver and got
into a fight, or something of the sorts, with another truck driver and lost
his leg. I never found out the real reason behind the missing leg. A lost

opportunity. Now, I talk to my doctor about what I need to do to prevent
getting diabetes. He tells me that the level of sugar in my blood is good.
Better than his. He says this with a smile. I do not trust his smile. I think

of my father and the many times I have given him rice, chicken, wine—
and everything that turns into sugar (it seems)—to eat. I think about the

times my father eats these things w/o me giving them to him. The doctor's
smile surfaces. It pulls at my fear. In a mocking way. I run from it, refusing
to face what it says.

The Case of Zen

The past sends stories along the wall
of thoughts. Light climbs down into
a boat near a bridge bending with the
weight of nothing.

This case of Zen does not end but
circles back to where it begins.
It is an act of revolution to think
without having told that the mind
can bend like a bridge whose weight is
nothing.

It pains the laborer to see leisure and
not feel it. He looks for ideas but none
has grown fruits in his life worth keeping.
The companion to the mundane is everything
that happens.

Hands lash against the wall and tear
it apart like the jaws of a hungry beast.
Thoughts pass like life into the great
beyond and growth often trails tears.

Can the dead see the living and know that
they are dead? The answer is in the
silence of everything.

Transgressing of Animals

In the beginning were a [man] and a woman.
Along came the snake and they gave birth to
wisdom.

There are two types of wisdom, hu[man] and
divine. Which one is pulling your coat, uncovering
your nakedness?

Sometimes, I hide in books. The pages are my
friends—they end like all relationships must end.

When I was a child, I would climb up the back of
my father and lay there still. He was the tallest
tree possible. The hair on his head was black
leaves. Now they are gray.

The earth trembles with the transgressing of
animals outside the garden, reprimanding the
seeker for seeking more than what is known,

than what becomes hu[man] when dust takes shape
in a shapeless universe.

Lunch Lady

I imagine her strong. I imagine her weak. This lunch
lady with Spanish rolling off her tongue like rivers.

The radio in the kitchen stays on evangelists that call their
flock. Shepards going after lost sheep with radio waves.

Who is coming to save her? Is anyone looking for her?

One day, I overheard her say the word cancer on the
phone, her Spanish unable to cover it from my ears. Or,
did I imagine this?

We talk food and family. She eats salads. Is a picky eater.
Her young daughter teaches in Korea and took a recent trip
to India.

There are grandchildren here in New York City. She spends time
with them and friends from church on the weekends.

I imagine a group of grandmothers walking the streets, the
weight of the world chipping from their backs.

They are in the sun. I cannot tell if they are walking toward it
or away from it. But it is shining.

The lunch lady has a life outside of the school's kitchen. She
has family. She has friends. She has learned to survive.

Rescue

I did not know my feelings until I named them, starting
with anger, the emperor of emotions—an attempt to not
make them get the best of me.

They came rushing in like waves. Visitors that do not stay
for long. In their wake, an archipelago of memories.

> I remember the leaving of the village. And the
> grief that it sprung. A web that tethered me to
> the dark days of youth.

My father stands in the kitchen past midnight most nights.
(He works the 3-11 PM shift and is home before midnight
most nights.) I can never tell what is on his mind. His
bloodshot eyes send me back to bed. I dream of silence in
silence.

Then there is fear overcome by confidence as I sit in class-
rooms of white faces at college.

I knew then, what I know now, that no one was coming to
rescue me.

Psychic Imprints/Recognition

I watch my mother belt a song on the
podium of the church in the village. She
sings it every Sunday.

Years later, I recognize the song as Simon
and Garfunkel's "Bridge Over Troubled Waters"

and am surprised by its allowance in a church
that championed the religious over the secular.

How can art transcend dichotomies? The
answer is in the message.

Control

She has fear in her eyes. Her son was diagnosed and recommended medication by someone who is not a therapist or doctor.

She asks for advice. I apologize—say that the teacher (a colleague) who diagnosed her son is wrong, outside of her league.

I spew that white students who
"act out" are labeled normal (they are kids being kids).
But that black and brown students are offered
medication to control them. She knows this.

It is the source of her fear. We talk about programs
outside of school to help her son advance. Her bright son.

I mention the Saturday program at the
Schomburg Center in Harlem, Prep for Prep,
and the Oliver Scholars program. She knows about these
and is looking into them. I promise to stay in touch.

Say that I am willing to help. She smiles. The fear gone, for now.

Facing Forward

Do you know where light goes when
you do not see it?

Look in the dark.
Let it envelop you like the womb.

When evil happens, God is pregnant with justice.
God is pregnant with justice, when evil happens.

Waiting to flood the world with justice, God is pregnant
when evil happens.

Faith is not in knowing.
It holds fast to uncertainties.

Faith holds fast to uncertainties, without knowing.

To believe that fear is an illusion is an illusion.

An illusion is that fear is an illusion.

Have more courage than fear. Courage is greater
than fear.

I Am Awake

I beg the stars to see the
day. They lend a helping
hand and I greet the sun.
Its smile a reflection of my
smile. I am alive and for
this I sing praise. Sweet
songs like honey in the
rock. I sway to the beat
of the rain against my skin.
I stand still and take it all
in—this majesty that is
nature. A queen that shows
her beauty and grace with
each waking moment.

Tsunami

Desertion as dislocation.
     In New Orleans, people ran with the flood,
afraid it would pull them to the earth's core.

*The skin can bear weight but is breakable.
     Be gentle with yourself and with others.
Carry a light load at all times, or none at all.

It is said that before a tsunami hits land, animals run
to safety before humans can figure out what is about
to happen—that water can climb the tallest wall with the
least amount of time.

The animals turn their nose to this. A challenge perhaps.
I can out smart you, before you know what I am doing.
Escape to safety. A home away from home.

*The skin is tough but breakable. And now is the
time to end this battle by declaring the self the winner.

NOTES

1. "Papa Legba" is a deity in religious traditions that originated in West Africa and are practiced globally in the African Diaspora. He is often invoked at the start of religious ceremonies.

2. "Arrival" is named after poet Cheryl Boyce-Taylor's collection *Arrival*. Cheryl is a dear mentor and friend.

3. "The Bridge" is in support of the ongoing campaign to rename the Williamsburg Bridge in New York City after the saxophonist Sonny Rollins.

4. "Rastaman Vibration" and "Positive Vibration" were written with the thoughts of Bob Marley's music in mind, especially his *Rastaman Vibration* album.

5. "Half Nelson" was inspired by a story in the jazz world about bassist Nelson Boyd who played, along with Miles Davis, on the song "Half Nelson" composed by Miles Davis. It is said that the song was named after Boyd because of his height.

6. "Made in DR" is not just about BBLs. It's about the interaction between cultural heritage and self-acceptance and how these two aspects drive each other at times.

7. "Saint Coltrane" pays homage to the spirituality of John Coltrane's music.

8. "Bend Down Low" is a song by Bob Marley on his *Natty Dread* album. The three poems that share this title conflate the biblical stories of Jesus conversing with a prostitute at a well and Jesus and his disciples plucking grain in the field on the Sabbath. The poems implicate one of the disciples (Peter) as sleeping with the woman. They also recall the washing of feet attributed to Jesus and as told in the Bible.

9. The asterisk (*) in "Tsunami" reinforces the importance of self-care.

ACKNOWLEDGMENTS

I am forever grateful to the editors of the following magazines for featuring some of the poems in this collection.

WordFest Anthology: "Primordial Orbits (Arrival)"
Ethel Magazine: "Harriet Tubman," "The Fire in My Brother"
Anti-Heroin Chic: "I Miss"
Pretty Cool Poetry Thing Magazine: "Dreams"
The Stay Project: "Politricks as Usual"
Setu Journal: "Conspiracy," "Love and Such," "Positive Vibration"
Amsterdam Quarterly: "For Victims of Natural Catastrophes," "The Search For Home"
"Unfinished Woman" was longlisted for The Show Me Yours Prize
The BeZine: "The Long History of Genocide," "Control"
Heat the Grease, We're Frying Up Some Poetry: "Lunch Lady"

Writing this book was a labor of love and I would not have finished it without the love and support of family and friends. Special thanks to: Marcel Alves, Shelly Alves, Dana Britton-Alves, Wynita Alves, Otis Alves, Maleeha, Malcolm, Jaedan, Dereyanah, O'ryan, Jacob, Malachi, Indira, Divine, Dylan, TJ, Tyler, Zayne, Mykah, The Britton Family, James Jones, Edmund James, Desiree Liverpool and Family, The Dixon Family, The Goodluck Family, The Ojevwe Family, Dionne Dixon and the boyz, Ann Fraser, Sigman David, Winston Williams and Family, LaVaughn Goodluck, Fidelis Ojevwe, Eugene "Bernie" Kendrick and Family, Sherri Matthews, Larry Berkowitz-Torres and Family, Eric White, Kwame

Hall, Marie-Laure Epaminondas, Shantel Hubert, Marcus Brock, Harvey Sindima, Margaret Darby, Tom Howard, Keisha-Gaye Anderson, Cheryl Boyce-Taylor, JP Howard, Amber Atiya, Cynthia Manick, Terence Culleton, Michelle Reale, Pangernungba Kechu and Family, Tishon Woolcock, Juliet Emanuel, and Lisa Moy.

I would also like to thank publisher Dr. Ross Tangedal, editor Eva Nielsen, and the entire staff of Cornerstone Press for helping to put this collection into the world.

Last but not least, if you read this book, thank you!

ELVIS ALVES was born in Guyana and raised in Brooklyn, New York. He is a graduate of Colgate University and Princeton Theological Seminary. His work has appeared in several journals and magazines including *Poetry, Sojourners, Transition, Caribbean Writer Journal,* and *StepAway Magazine.* He is the author of *Bitter Melon* (2013), *Ota Benga* (2017), *I Am No Battlefield But A Forest Of Trees Growing* (winner of the Jacopone da Todi Poetry Book Prize, 2018), *Black/White: We Are Not Panic (Pandemic) Free* (2020), *Blackfish* (2022), and *This Is What I Know* (2023).

www.elvisalves.com

www.ingramcontent.com/pod-product-compliance
Lightning Source LLC
Chambersburg PA
CBHW031444120626
46545CB00006B/2543